WELCOME TO WHIGVILLE

A MEMOIR

BOB BUREK

HIDDEN HOLLOWS PUBLISHING

ISBN 978-1-7323579-6-9

eISBN 978-1-7323579-7-6

Hidden Hollows Publishing
Flint MI

CONTENTS

Dedicated to Sally Burek

The Love of My Life

ACKNOWLEDGMENTS

I would be remiss in not recognizing the contributions of two people in the writing of this book.

The first is Karen Healy, my secretary and co-worker in my years as Superintendent of the Fenton Area Public Schools. No "boss" ever had a more competent, dedicated or loyal co-worker. In this effort, Karen performed more than putting text on paper. She offered suggestions at every turn, encouraged me to complete the work and, as she did so efficiently during our years in Fenton, she never missed a deadline.

The second person in this support system is Dr. Dallas Gatlin, a student at Grand Blanc High School in my years there as an Assistant Principal. A gifted writer in his own right, Dallas was a motivational force in my writing of this book. More than encouraging me to take on this effort, Dallas became my unofficial support system in its completion. As I progressed through this writing, he would offer ideas and suggestions. His critique was invaluable. It is not a stretch to say that without his ongoing assistance, I seriously doubt I would have completed the book. To him, I owe much.

PROLOGUE

WHY WOULD a man in his eighties write a book for the first time? The answer is partly in the math. I am in my 80s with life closing in, and I want to offer my life story to my children and grandchildren so that they can understand in part where they came from. Hopefully, each of them can take a piece of me with them as they progress through their own lives.

A second reason is the passing of my closest friend in life, Jim Robinson. "Robby" passed away two years ago. Detailed in this book is a story of our friendship from our first encounter in the second grade to the life story we shared over a period of eight decades. His leaving this earth was a jolt to my system, and I began to recognize my own mortality.

Finally, I wanted to offer a "hats off" to Whigville, a residential neighborhood 10 miles south of Flint, Michigan, and part of the community of Grand Blanc. To parrot an old saying, "You can take the boy out of

Whigville but can't take Whigville out of the boy." Whigville, with its dirt roads, creek, fields, and ball diamonds forged out of raw acreage was the story of my youth in the 1940s and '50s. I never forgot where I came from, and I want in this book to recognize its importance to kids of that era.

1

MOM AND ME

IT ALL BEGAN SO SIMPLY. I was born in Flint, Michigan, at Hurley Hospital on November 2, 1940 to Peter and Mary Burek. My only sibling, Barbara, had joined the family four years before. My father worked production at Chevrolet Motors, one of the huge automotive production facilities in Flint. Our family of four lived in a quaint, heavily Polish neighborhood in the north end of Flint. Ours was a modest yet respectable life with a steady income earned by my father. In those days, dads worked and mothers stayed at home. That began to change for many, however, after December 7, 1941, when the Japanese attacked our naval base at Pearl Harbor on the island of Oahu. Roosevelt quickly declared war on Japan and, soon after, on Germany. In Flint and other industrial towns, women were recruited to work in wartime factories as the demand increased for more and more workers to fill the needs of those wartime factories. My mother, however, chose to remain at home. This was a great benefit to my sister and me.

It wasn't long after the declaration of war that my father was transferred to a munitions factory in Detroit. Our family joined him early in 1942. My memories of those early years are actually quite vivid, though I was not yet five years old. In those years, I was definitely a mama's boy. I was tied to her "at the hip."

The war changed everything, but for a boy it was just the way it was, and I can look back now on how my mother navigated it all. I have a strong memory of standing in long lines with my mother as she exchanged, as I later learned, what were government issued stamps for food commodities like sugar and flour, plus gasoline and other scarce items. I remember many shopping trips to downtown Detroit. We rode the bus, as my mother never drove. We lived on Six Mile Road, so the bus trip was relatively short. A reward on occasions for enduring those shopping trips was attending a movie at the Fisher Theater which, at that time, was set up for movies only. Even more exciting was the annual Christmas visit to the famous Hudson's Department Store. I believe the third floor of the building in December was dedicated to Christmas décor and, of course, a place for Santa Claus. It was a fairy-tale experience for a young boy. My sister was, of course, green with envy. Mom would return to Hudson's on the weekend so Barb could make her case with Santa Claus. My mom always made things work, always balanced things out. She loved us and we knew it.

Soon it was time for me to start school in Detroit. I also remember refusing to attend the opening of school in the fall as a kindergartener. The school was one block from our house. As school started, my mother would walk me to school in the morning whereupon, despite her pleading, I would follow her back home. The "protest" lasted a week before I was convinced by two adults, teacher and mother, that attending school was in my best interest. Little did I know then that school and education were to become the center of my life.

I have great memories of those early years in Detroit. Our neighborhood along Six Mile was absolutely saturated with children, children of all ages. Friends were easy to find and to connect with. There was always something going on in the neighborhood. Halloween was an absolute blast, because families were packed in the area and candy was bountiful. Finally, I remember having a "thing" about animals. I loved animals of all stripes...dogs, cats, squirrels, birds, bunnies. When I found a "road kill," I arranged a proper burial with a grave and cross. Our back yard had a small cemetery before my mother squelched that idea.

In 1945, our lives changed again. The war was over. My father was transferred back to Flint at Chevrolet Motors. In the first few months, my dad lived with his mother in Flint while we remained in Detroit. He would come home on weekends. Shortly after the first of the year, in 1946, our family moved to Grand Blanc. Actually, we moved to a residential area of Grand Blanc named Whigville. Our community was about 10 miles south of Flint. Historically, dating back to the mid-1800s, the Grand Blanc area was heavily invested in farming, but after World War II the economy shifted as family farms began to disappear and manufacturing became the economic engine of the community. My father was a dedicated employee in this engine.

I really didn't know my father in those "growing up" years. I don't offer this as an indictment of him. I didn't consider him a bad person. He worked eight to ten hours a day, seven days a week. All for the sake of his family. Compounding the situation, he worked the second shift at what the locals called Chevy in the Hole. Because he was at work from early afternoon until midnight, my sister Barbara and I were sleeping when he got home and at school when he woke up. As a result, he missed attending the activities of two very active children.

I was involved in sports in middle school and high school, yet my father never attended a single contest in which I played. Our contact was limited to those weekend days that he did not work, usually just Sundays. My father was a bit like a phantom in those K-12 years. My sister and I needed him, we loved him, but we really didn't know him. This, by the way, wasn't uncommon. Many of my friends had lived a similar experience with a "no show" dad. It's just the way it was.

My mother, on the other hand, was the ever-present, deeply loved, heart of our family. She single-handedly raised my sister and me. She was there in the morning to ensure we had a warm meal and a packed lunch to take to school. She was there in the afternoon when I returned home from school. When school functions required a parent to be present, such as parent-teacher conferences, she would *walk* the three miles to school to support my sister and me! This included attendance at sports activities in which I was involved. Again, she had to walk to school to watch her son play—and she did, without fail.

Some neighborly kindness finally came to her aid after my freshman year in high school, in the form of a schoolmate's parents. They gave my mother a ride to these functions since he and I were involved in the same sports. It was a great and appreciated gesture, and yet I knew, ride or not, my mom was going to be there. No mother was more dedicated to her children than she was!

Mom also made sure we had clean clothes and good food. I recall that our food was very simple. There were three criteria my mother followed in feeding us: (1) It had to be inexpensive (cheap!) to purchase, (2) it had to be filling, and (3) it had to be reasonably tasteful. Breakfast for me was usually oatmeal and toast. Once in a while I had pancakes. My sister liked French toast and, since I detested the smell of it, I stayed upstairs until she finished eating. Dinner was usually some form of hamburger and included goulash, chili, meatloaf and sloppy joes. Pasta and chicken were less frequent items on the menu. My school lunch always included a bologna or Spam sandwich, an apple, pear or peach, and a cookie. Mom's oatmeal cookies were and are my all-time favorite. I bought milk at school at 5¢ a carton.

We ate breakfast and dinner at a set time for the three of us. My dad's work schedule only allowed him to eat with us on Sunday, so it was my sister, mother and me at the dinner table. This all changed, of course, when we got to high school with the crazy schedule of sports, practices and other school activities.

No boy had a better mother (Mary).

When I entered high school, my practice schedule got me home at odd times, so my mother would set out a card table on which I would eat dinner and do my homework while she washed my sports clothing. Later, when we bought a television, I would eat, do my homework and watch an occasional TV program.

My clothes were very simple by today's standards. I rotated two pairs of blue jeans and three shirts...long-sleeve shirts in the late fall and winter and short-sleeve shirts the rest of the school year. A sociologist would have labeled us as lower middle class. My sister and I didn't give much thought to our socio-economic status. All we knew was that our parents loved us—dad through work and mom through loving nurture.

In my pre-K years, my sister, Barbara, terrorized me as only an older sister can (she also loved me). I have three very distinct memories of my interactions with her. One, she dressed me as a girl with various clothes she cobbled up, insisting that I remain silent and standing as she prepared me for a "fashion show." Two, she would loan me money for some item that I wanted but with interest charged, a due date for repaying the loan, and a signature by our mother, backing up repayment of the loan. All of this was, of course, documented in a "contract" spelling out these conditions. Three, I was forced to sing Christmas carols in front of her. She would then rate my performance on a 1-10 scale with 10 being best. The only song that got me a score at the top of the scale was "Silent Night." I could belt it out pretty good. All the other songs got dismal ratings. Needless to say, all of this was very demeaning.

I will say, however, that later in my middle school years, when she was in high school, I returned her early manipulation of me in spades. I was the proverbial pest when she was with her girlfriends or with one of her boyfriends. I would listen in on a phone extension when she talked to a girlfriend or boyfriend and "blackmail" her with the information I had about some juicy item. My sister christened me "brat!" Our irritated mom played referee.

Shortly after moving to Whigville (Grand Blanc), my dad had a brainstorm that almost destroyed my mother. He decided to build a grocery store on our property, despite the fact that there were two other grocery stores in the immediate area. My father saw this as a way to leave the grind of the assembly line and retire at a relatively young age. The problem was that he expected his wife to operate the store in addition to raising two very active and involved kids and manage a house. At launch, she became the sole employee of the "Whigville Shopping Center." I remember with fondness my mother and I (her helper) operating the store while listening to Detroit Tigers and Detroit Red Wings games while sipping on a Pepsi, my favorite soda. How my mother did what she did in those years and retain her sanity is a mystery to my sister and me.

And there was still a house to keep. Barbara and I were given very specific duties around the house. In my instance, for whatever reason, my dad wrote out my jobs on paper. Those tasks were to be accomplished when not at school or working in the store to assist mom. For Barbara, helping to wash and iron clothes, vacuuming the floor and dusting the furniture were the chief duties. For me, taking out the garbage and doing yard work (mowing, trimming, and raking the lawn clippings) were the jobs dad set out. My sister and I argued over washing the dishes. Neither one of us wanted to dry the dishes. She, of course, as the more senior partner, won out. I dried the dishes.

Relative to discipline, there were very clear expectations with consequences if we crossed the line. Our language, work habits, and obedience to our parents were among the expectations laid out by our mother and father. My mother never laid a hand on me. My dad did so on rare occasions. Many in my generation, especially the boys, lived in a more physical environment where spankings with a belt or a board were a dad's response if one violated the rules. My dad liked to cuff me across the back of my head if I crossed the line. Immediately, my mother came to my defense and loudly chastised my father and told him to keep his hands off me!

As one reads this chapter, my expectation is that the reader gets a clear impression that my mother raised me, supported me and defended me. The same with my sister. We later came to know our dad's love was there all the time, even when he wasn't there. But mom's love was always present and obvious—deep, dependable, undeniable.

I should note that my dad became a father to me

the closer I got to graduation from high school. By that time, he was close to retirement and was working fewer hours and never on weekends. He was reaching for the coveted "30-and-out." With Saturdays free, he would take me to Flint to purchase supplies for the grocery store. He would run into his co-workers on the streets in Flint, and he genuinely was proud to introduce me as his son. I really felt good about his change in demeanor toward me.

The good story continues. By the time I went to college, he had done his time in "The Hole" and retired from Chevrolet Motors. My parents would visit me on occasion in Mount Pleasant at Central Michigan University. My father was a good athlete in his day, and he loved watching me play varsity baseball in college. In so many ways, he demonstrated his pride in seeing his only son play and excel at college baseball. The day I was selected as the team captain for my senior year, he broke down crying on the phone as I relayed the information to him. Granted, all of his attention came late, but nonetheless I treasured this newfound connection with my dad. Still later when I married, and we had children, he was the "grandfather of the year" each and every year to our three daughters! He and my mother doted on them which made their son and daughter-in-law very happy. They only lived four miles away, so the contact was frequent with the girls all the way through their graduation from high school. Sally and I treasured those years and the strength of the relationship with my parents. They were truly great years as a family.

My father was an incessant shopper in his retirement years. He would go to Kmart, Sam's or any other "Big Box" retailer to purchase large quantities of consumable goods necessary to keep a family functioning. Items like toilet paper, paper towels, Kleenex were popular. On the food side, he would load up on fruit juice, hot dogs, crackers and many other commodities. His children were the recipients of his newfound hobby. Most trips to our house carried with him many of the products named above. They would quickly go to storage in our basement. Whatever his motivation, the result was actually a boon to our everyday needs. He also loved going to garage sales where he eventually bought items that in reality no one could use, but the motivation was on target. What a dad!

Looking back, things were not always perfect—they were better than perfect. They were formative! Through opportunities and real-life challenges, through a war and its impact on my family and friends, we all grew a little every day in Flint, through Detroit, and finally to Whigville, a magical little "world in between" that lives in my memories as *The Neighborhood.*

2

THE NEIGHBORHOOD

FOLLOWING the conclusion of World War II, my father, Peter Burek, moved our family from Detroit, Michigan, where he worked in a munitions factory, to Grand Blanc. We moved to a modest yet idyllic residential neighborhood located two miles north of Grand Blanc named Whigville. Our little slice of Whigville consisted of six dirt roads off a four-lane artery named Dort Highway. Each dirt road carried the title of "Heights," with ours being "Strong Heights." The "Heights" in order from north to south were Kettering, Sloan, Durant, Strong, Baker and Fisher, and the Heights were filled with school-aged kids who, when they were home, played from dusk till dawn!

My father, like the majority of fathers in our neighborhood, worked for General Motors' Chevrolet. Flint was to become in 25 years the nation's auto capital, with over 80,000 hourly employees in the late 1970s.

1946

Bob and Corky in Whigville

The families of Whigville consisted of working dads and stay-at-home mothers. My father was employed at Chevrolet Motors working the 2:30 p.m.-11:00 p.m. shift six or seven days a week. As a kid, I rarely saw him. My go-to parent was my mother, Mary, who, like all moms in the area, was a stay-at-home mom. Though I gave it no thought at the time, in contrast to today's single-parent families, almost all the homes in the Heights had both parents in place and the neighborhood was "family."

Growing up in such a "family" had consequences! The fact that moms were at home full time and were connected with other moms in the neighborhood created a little problem for the kids. News of any altercation or serious issue involving two or more of us seemed to travel faster than the speed of light to every mother of every kid in the neighborhood. All the details were furnished in glorious description. My mother somehow knew all the details about what happened before I even got home—or at least it seemed like it! A special nemesis of mine was an older lady by the name of Milly Stahly. She had an uncanny knack of knowing everything I did that I shouldn't have and, always in quick order, shared the necessary details with my mother. On the other hand, those same ladies—even Milly—were our protectors and would intervene on our behalf if, for example, an older teenager would pick on one of us. The parents and kids in Whigville practiced their own sort of social justice, and most the time it all evened out and worked out for the best!

There were kids and kids and more kids of all ages in Whigville! I never lacked for friends or playmates. We also never lacked for things to do. Bicycling, "kick the can," hide-and-seek and rubber gun fights were among the things to do for the younger kids.

My buddies were essentially my age with a few notable exceptions. Several boys in their early teens would stop by at least once a week asking my mother if "Bobby" could come out to play. I was eight or nine at the time this ritual started. In short, they didn't really want me. They wanted my sports equipment. My parents made sure I had baseballs and a bat, a football, a basketball and a hockey stick and puck. Of course, the deal I made was I had to play or they didn't get my equipment. As it turned out, this made me a better athlete as I moved into my teens and later.

Competing with the older guys honed my skills and love for competition—an advantage that paid dividends in high school and college and even in later life.

I was blessed with good friends in my youth. Three deserve special attention. Ron Darnell was a year younger than me and a very good athlete for his size. Ron still lives today in the house where he grew up in the 1950s. Eugene Hubbard, a year older than me, distinguished himself as an All-State football lineman at Grand Blanc High School, and later, as an All-American offensive guard at Hillsdale College. The third person was my neighbor across the street, Sandy Schanick. She was definitely a "tom boy." She was a fierce rival throughout my childhood, especially in basketball, and she could play with the best of the boys. Because she lived so close, we had many a battle. Sadly for me, she won most of them. But I went away from each one with a new lesson learned for future competitions and a healthy respect for girls!

Whigville had much to commend it. However, in contrast to outstanding facilities for sports competitions in most suburban areas today, ours were almost primitive. The gravel road was our football field, and the goalposts were garbage cans. A basket on a pole or nailed above a garage door served us for basketball games. The pond at the end of the street was our hockey arena and a baseball diamond forged out of a field two streets down was our sandlot. Since we didn't know any better, we were more than satisfied with our "facilities."

We were always outdoors, irrespective of the time

of year. That meant after school during the year and all the time in the summer! The only time I was indoors was to eat, sleep, and later in high school, do homework. Television wasn't a part of my generation's world until the mid-1950s and then only for a few families. If a family had a television in the early 1950s, that meant the kid came from affluence. There was no affluence in Whigville!

Thread Creek was good to Bob.

Besides the competitive games, there was the availability of fields and a creek. Thread Creek captured my attention and that of my friends early in our youth. It was located a quarter mile due east of our house. It was a paradise of riches for kids. We swam and fished in it. In the winter, we skated on it and trapped for muskrat and mink. My dear mother accompanied me on my early 5:00 a.m. check of the traps to see if we were lucky with a catch. She was so afraid that I would fall through the ice. On one occasion, what I thought was a dead muskrat was a live one. When I confidently reached into the water to retrieve the muskrat, he sprang up and latched onto my leg. I still have the scar today. Of course, my mother was yelling at me to "kill the rat." A tetanus shot followed. I was back in school the next morning.

This was a lucrative business for a kid. Muskrat pelts sold for $1.75, mink for $18.00. I would normally get 40-50 pelts each winter. That was gold for a kid in the 1950s.

A real source of pride was the treehouse my buddies and I built just off the creek. It was constructed about 20 feet off the ground in a very large oak tree. The height of the structure enabled us to scan the countryside for would be intruders - or the owner of the farm.

The creek and field were part of a farm owned by a Mr. Evatt. Whenever he saw us on his property, his first instinct was to yell at us to leave his property. On rare occasions, he would try to chase us down, but no 40-year-old is ever going to catch any self-respecting 10-year-old, even on his best day. Actually, I don't think he ever wanted to catch us. We were no threat to him or the farm. I returned each spring to walk the property, visit the fishing spots and view the tree-house. It was a ritual I so looked forward to. This came with the consent of Mr. Evatt's daughter, Ginny, who runs the farm today with her husband. The treehouse lasted for 50 years before weather and the elements took it down a decade ago.

There is a great follow-up to the Evatt farm story. Years later, I attended Grand Blanc High School with Mr. Evatt's oldest daughter, Peggy. Still later, when I was Principal of Grand Blanc High School, Peggy's siblings were students in the building. I was good to them!

In the summer years of my youth from age nine or 10 until age 15, I was involved in competitive baseball in Flint. We formed a team from all over Whigville. By this time, my father had built a grocery store on our property. He sponsored our team with "Whigville Shopping Center" on the T-shirts. Almost every day we rode our bikes to the closest baseball diamond in Flint, McKinley Elementary, which was seven to eight miles away. This would be unthinkable in today's world, because we rode our bikes on the four-lane highway most of the way. Once there, we played an organized game in the morning with pick-up games the rest of the day. The only stipulation from home was "be back by 5:00 p.m.!" One did not violate these directions. It is worth noting that the championship baseball team that I played on in high school had its roots in those sandlot teams of the early 1950s.

As I approached the middle school years, I joined the 4-H Garden Club. Our sponsor was an agriculture teacher from the high school. Grand Blanc was an agricultural community from the second half of the

19th century up to the 1960s, when farms became sub-divisions and the economy of the entire region shifted to automotive production.

My little garden, perhaps 12 feet by 30 feet, included tomatoes, radishes, carrots and beans. Every summer we showed our produce in a 4-H Fair held at the high school. Our 4-H advisor was a man named Joe Jewett. He was a tremendous man and made me feel really good about my 4-H fair entry. Every summer he would stop by our house two or three times to offer suggestions on my garden. I always looked forward to the visit because he was so positive. He was a radiant and positive human being. I wouldn't have used those words then, but I'm certain I felt his interest and kindness. This stuck with me and I'm sure has influenced my approach to relationships and mentoring along the way.

There was one major disruption to our lives late in my elementary years. As I mentioned, my folks—and by folks, I mean my dad—decided to build a grocery store on our property facing Dort Highway as an enabler to leave his job at Chevrolet Motors (which he did not like) and move into retirement with income from the store.

There were a couple problems with this decision. First, there were two other grocery stores on Dort Highway within 150 yards of our proposed building. Second, he never consulted my mother on this decision. She was to run the store in addition to raising two kids and managing a household. It did, however, become a social hangout for many of the ladies in the neighborhood. They loved my mother and on numerous occasions walked to the store to buy a couple items as an excuse to pay her a visit. Due to my mother's popularity, there was always someone in the store "shooting the breeze."

As for me, I actually liked the store. In addition to scooping ice cream (5 cents a single dip and 10 cents for a double) for people of all ages, my first stop after getting off the bus at the end of the school day was to get a bottle of soda or a candy bar. Visits to the dentist no doubt increased as a result of our owning this grocery store! This era ended when my parents sold the store and our house to a credit union when I left for my freshman year in college. They moved into a very nice house on the west side of Grand Blanc.

I can't leave the story here without telling you about the diner located just south of us on the highway. It was a malt and burger place frequented by teenagers in the area. The place was off limits for the younger crowd when teenagers were in the place. The pecking order was rigidly in place and all the kids knew it. Every once in a while my mother would give me a half dollar to buy a burger (25 cents), French fries (10 cents) and a Pepsi (10 cents). That was the cost of doing business back then. Lots of things happened there—lots of camaraderie, conflicts, and conflict resolution—lots of growing up in Whigville.

So the neighborhood was the center of the universe for me growing up in the 1940s and '50s. Those were simple times. No cell phones, no television, no reason to stay in the house. You played, forged friendships and alliances, and worked out disagreements without an adult referee. You literally found out who you were, formed an identity, became a teenager with somewhat of a game plan for your life. Whigville is where I moved from childhood to teenager to a young adult with plans for college all occurring in 12 years.

This little village, this unique collection of special people clearly defined me...moved me to independent thinking and acting, and gave me direction in life. One created his own destiny in those years in the care of community. You might choose to build cars for 30 years, or houses, or nurture students as an educator—so many choices, so much support, so many experiences. Loyalty was the currency for a relationship. Friendships were for life in many cases. If you got knocked down, there was also a cheering section or the help needed to get back up.

It may be strange to some, but I return to the old neighborhood in the "Heights" at least once every two months. I have done this my entire adult life. I drive up and down the streets of the "Heights" to connect to my youth. There are so many memories tied into each of those streets and the people who lived on them. Whigville was literally my life from ages 6-18, and while on the "tour" I recall so many families who lived there. So many kids, so many memories. Among other things, it has kept me grounded as I became successful in my life and career, living in bigger homes with more worldly possessions. I believe I am and have been the same person all the years of my adult life as I was in the 1940s and 1950s. I credit that, in part, to the "tour."

My loyalty to Whigville remains as strong today as it was in the 1950s. It is part of my very fiber. All of this early history in my life and the people in it enabled me, a son of Whigville, to be successful as a professional and as a husband and father. And yet I need you to know, these formative years would never have been enough, had it not been for a serendipitous meeting with a girl in a sweater. The air filled with spring lilacs, and my eyes and heart filled with her.

3

THE LAVENDER SWEATER

My wife of 61 years and I first met late in the second semester of our sophomore year at Central Michigan University. Sally Cooper and I were closing out our second year at CMU. The year was 1960. I first saw her late one afternoon that spring. She was sitting with a group of girls in the Student Union. I was walking through the Union on the way to my dormitory after baseball practice. Sally was wearing a lavender sweater and skirt. She was an attractive girl and, as I approached her table, our eyes met briefly. I recall that she was the center of the chatter. It was clear that everything about her was upbeat. A slender girl with a constant smile, she radiated warmth, support and caring, all trademarks of a personality I came to know. There was something about her and that moment, our first "meeting," that really resonated with me.

At that time, besides academics, the only item on my agenda was baseball. I was completing my first year on the varsity baseball team and having a great season. Girls were simply not on my agenda...that is, until I saw Sally. As I left the Union, I said to myself, "I want to meet this girl." I did not know her name or the residence hall in which she lived, but these were minor details given the smallness of the CMU campus.

Somehow in the next week, I was able to get her name, and, through mutual friends, a first date was arranged. As I remember, her roommate (soon to be CMU's Homecoming Queen) set up our first meeting. We met at a malt and burger place just north of the campus. Our date was a little awkward at first, but her personality quickly got us over the hump. I was a skinny 5' 9"and a man of few words, especially around girls. Sally was poles opposite with a dynamite personality and a constant smile. She carried our conversation that day and each day going forward. That day marked the beginning of my personality conversion, at least around girls. With Sally, I became more confident and engaging in our increasing number of contacts. Simply put, Sally brought me out of my shyness.

I soon found out that Sally loved to eat. The pizza we ordered had eight pieces. I distinctly remember that this amazingly fit and beautiful girl ate five pieces and lovingly looked at a sixth (which was to be my third piece). She attacked the food like there was no tomorrow. I was definitely "on guard" for future dinner dates. I probably grimaced a little at that time because my financial resources were limited. It would be a challenge to keep the price of our next and future meals within my budget. In all seriousness however, we had a great time with lots of laughs and, most importantly, we agreed that we wanted to see each other again.

Unfortunately, there was little time left in the school year. I was really involved in baseball with multiple games on the schedule and frequent road trips. We saw each other only a few additional times that spring. Sally was soon to head for home and a summer job with the Muskegon Chronicle. I was going home to Grand Blanc and a job with Consumers Power. We had minimal contact that summer, but we knew that we wanted to see each other again in the fall.

There was so much about Sally Cooper that I liked. She was beautiful, personality plus, positive, upbeat, caring and oh so much fun to be with. I knew she cared as much about me. As the semester came to a close, we didn't say much about our feelings, but I knew I was clearly falling for this girl. In hindsight, I never had a serious relationship with any other young lady. I dated a number of girls but didn't have a "steady girlfriend," never liked one girl in particular. Every girl I dated was measured by how they stacked up against my mother, a woman I respected and adored. My mom was caring, upbeat, positive and personable. Sound familiar? On the other hand, as I found out later, Sally had a steady boyfriend most of her four years in high school. I do not remember our having much contact over that summer. Perhaps a few telephone calls and a few notes/letters, but that was the extent of it. Unfortunately, there were no cell phones.

When school resumed in the fall of our junior year, however, we immediately got back in touch, and our relationship blossomed. Neither of us had much money to do things that carried a significant price tag. I had a job with the sports department that brought me a few dollars each week, and Sally worked in food service in the dormitory. The lack of money, however, was no obstacle to our seeing each other. We spent most evenings studying in one of the two dorms or at the library. On weekends, there were social events in the dorm or athletic contests or college entertainment which we frequented. Once in a while, we would walk to Mt. Pleasant to see a movie. Mass was a must on Sunday. Sally is a deeply religious person. We were inseparable throughout our junior year. I knew very soon that I was falling in love with her and wanted nothing but to be with her. We began getting serious about our relationship and talked frequently about it. Something special was definitely happening.

In the second half of our junior year, some important things tied to our relationship began to happen. I had earlier in the fall joined a fraternity, Sigma Phi Epsilon. When a SPE had a serious relationship with a girl, the boy asked the girl if she would agree to be "pinned." In the process, a SPE pin is placed on the girl by the young man. In fraternity language, this was often the step prior to being engaged to be married. I asked Sally if she would agree to be pinned. She immediately said "yes." Thereafter, a springtime early-evening event took place outside her dormitory. All 50 of my fraternity brothers were present. They sang a very moving song called "My Sigma Phi Epsilon Sweetheart." A large crowd of onlookers was present as well as spectators watching from their dorm windows. It was truly a special event. The ceremony meant a great deal to each of us. We openly expressed our feelings for each other after the Sigma Phi event. We were inseparable from that point.

CMU Baseball Co-Captains Bob Burek and Sam Licavoli with Coach Bill Theunissen 1961-'62

Baseball continued to be a large part of my life. Workouts for the 1961 season began in December, and by January, the players who would go with the team on the southern trip were notified by the coach. I was selected as one of the captains and took my job seriously. I had a great season, although not as good as my sophomore year. It was becoming clear to me that I wasn't going to play major league baseball, a lifetime goal. In the last series of the year, we travelled to Eastern Michigan University for three games over the weekend. In the final game of the series, I stole home and broke the school record for runs scored and stolen bases. Unfortunately, I broke my leg on the steal to home. I was in the hospital for three days and the team returned to Mt. Pleasant.

I wanted in the worst way to hear from Sally, but there was no response from Mt. Pleasant. When I returned to campus with a cast and crutches, Sally came over immediately. She confessed that she had gone home that weekend to see her high school boyfriend. In tears, she admitted that she shouldn't have done it. She said she "simply wanted to confirm" that I was the right choice. Sally apologized profusely and asked for forgiveness. I was stunned. I said very little, and our meeting broke up. It took a few days for me to respond and when I did, I said, "Let's move on." That was the only downer in our relationship.

That summer we were in nonstop contact...calls, letters and visits to each other's home. By that time, our parents were well aware of how serious we were about each other. A weekend bus trip to Muskegon was a difficult one because of the cast and crutches. As it turned out, I was very comfortable with her parents and sister. I especially liked her dad. In turn, her visit to Grand Blanc also went well. My parents were enamored with Sally. My sister was married and no longer in the house. My dad especially liked Sally. That feeling never changed.

As we began our senior year, we were clearly in love with each other. Being with Sally was the most important part of my day. We were inseparable. I knew she was going to be my wife following our last year at CMU. The timing I wasn't sure of. We plodded through fall and as we approached the holiday season, I determined that I would pop the question at that time. I traveled to Muskegon the week before Christmas for a few days with Sally and her family. On Christmas Eve, 1961, I told her we should drive around Muskegon to see the outdoor Christmas displays which were a hallmark of that city. Later, Sally told me she knew I was going to ask her that night to marry... which I did on a hill overlooking Lake Michigan. Sally accepted and we immediately went back to her house to share the news with her parents and to call mine. Those were exciting times.

The second half of our senior year was a rush to graduation. My final season in baseball was literally playing on one leg. I never fully recovered from breaking my leg the previous year. After a couple of weeks, I went to Coach Theunissen, who I deeply respected, and asked him to move a teammate into my position. I served as an assistant coach that season and loved the experience! Coach Theunissen and I, by the way, became friends for life. He managed to find out about every "downturn" in my life and would send a letter of encouragement. I never figured out how he knew of my situation.

Sally and Bob circa 1962

We were to be married August 18, 1962. Sally worked hard that spring to secure a teaching position for the fall. She landed one in Clare, a small town 15 miles north of Mt. Pleasant. I was offered a graduate assistantship for the 1962-63 academic year in which I could work on my master's degree and teach and coach for the University. We received our undergraduate degrees in June, 1962. With a wedding almost three months away, Sally went home to Muskegon to work again at the Chronicle. I hired in at Chevrolet Motors in Flint. Working overtime I made (for me) incredible money. For a brief time, I questioned why I wanted to enter the teaching profession. After a month, despite the money, I had my answer. Working on the assembly line for 50 hours a week was not for me.

The magic time finally arrived! We exchanged vows on August 18. Our honeymoon was a blur. One of our honeymoon experiences still brings a chuckle today. On our trip to New York City, we stopped at Cooperstown, New York, home of the Major League Baseball Hall of Fame. On our way to the Hall, we passed the historical district of the town. There were a number of houses lived in by the founding fathers of Cooperstown. One of them belonged to the famous American author, James Fenimore Cooper. Included in his great writings was *The Last of the Mohicans*. Sally's family on her dad's side were actually descendants of this man. Sally, of course, was excited to visit the home. The charge was incredibly only 50 cents a person. I said it wasn't worth the cost and told her we should move on, so we did. Dutifully, she agreed. We pressed on to the Hall of Fame. The cost: $1.00 a person. I said, "Let's go." We did so with a few dirty looks sent my way. I got some measure of redemption a few years later when we went to New York and saw Barbra Streisand on Broadway.

After our honeymoon, it was back to Mt. Pleasant and a final year at CMU, as Sally taught first grade and I taught physical education classes and coached freshmen football and baseball while working on my master's degree. We moved into married housing. There were lots of young married couples in positions similar to ours. We truly loved that year and the relationships we formed. The 1962-63 year was a fun one for these newlyweds. Life was a little difficult for Sally on the professional side. Clare was a small town with a big heart, but most of her first graders had few cultural and social experiences and were lacking in learning skills. For example, none of them had ever been to a restaurant, so Sally arranged for a field trip to a local restaurant and gave them an introduction to social etiquette and manners. For those seven year olds it was a whole new world.

At Christmas time, Sally coerced me (using the James Fenimore Cooper story) into being Santa Claus. I dressed up like the big guy and, at the defined moment, walked into the auditorium surprising the entire school, who were involved in a holiday assembly. I bellowed a "Ho, Ho, Ho" from the back of the auditorium. The kids were stunned...for a brief moment. They recovered quickly, however, and then over a hundred of them stormed over me. That's 200 footprints of little seven-year-olds, and I can still feel footprints on my chest!!! The place was bedlam. What a great experience for them and me.

Compounding her first year difficulties was that she was pregnant and didn't know it right away. Life for me was much easier. While pursuing my master's degree, I worked as a teacher in the morning and a coach in the afternoon. The grad assistantship was in physical education while my undergrad major was in history, soon to be my high school teaching assignment. My advisor (bless his soul) allowed me to take most of my classes in U.S. History. The whole situation was a win-win for me. I received financial help to secure my Master's with coursework in my undergrad major.

My teaching assignment as the feature of my grad assistantship was bowling, an activity credit that was part of an undergraduate degree program at CMU. I taught 10 hours of bowling at a local bowling alley. The problem was I had never bowled in my life. I dutifully wrote the Brunswick Bowling Company with my dilemma. They, in turn, sent me a book on how to teach bowling. Also, I started bowling that summer.

When I met my first class in the fall, I carried out my instruction on how to grip the ball, the footwork involved and the release of the ball. Most of the class was girls plus a smattering of boys, all with limited or no experience...save one. His name was Mario. It turns out he was a great bowler; he averaged close to 200 a game and competed around the state. He suggested that he would be glad to step in, albeit a student, to assist. I readily agreed and he became the grad assistant's #1 assistant!

Soon we found out for sure that the Bureks were expecting their first child. Now it was paramount for me to complete my degree and for us to get jobs. We began in earnest after the holidays to do just that. At that time, it was truly a buyer's market. Teaching jobs were easy to find.

We briefly flirted with the thought of moving to California where beginning teacher salaries were several hundred dollars higher than Michigan, but of course, the grandparents-to-be would have none of that. We soon were offered and agreed to a teaching position in my hometown of Grand Blanc. Sally received an elementary assignment, and I took a position at Grand Blanc High School, my alma mater. The job offer was made by my former high school principal, Ms. Hazel Dowd. Our starting salaries for the 1963-64 school years were $5,200. I got an extra $200 for coaching junior varsity baseball!

We labored through the spring of 1963. These were "heady times." Sally was really the one financing our marriage. She made the money. My grad assistantship did not get us much money, but it did get me a master's degree and a bargaining chip with possible employers.

I completed the requirements for my advanced degree in August. With our new jobs beginning in a month, we rented a U-Haul, packed our few belongings and a one-month-old baby girl, said goodbye to friends and faculty and headed 90 miles south to Grand Blanc. A new life full of new people, adventures, and challenges was about to begin!

4

CLASSMATES AND MENTORS

PEOPLE of all ages had a profound and lasting impact on me in my teen years. There were classmates, team-mates—and in the grand scheme of life, there were mentors, although we didn't call them that at the time. I'm referring to high school teachers and coaches who guided, directed and supported my growth and aspi-rations.

In the late 1950s, Grand Blanc High School was the focal point of my life; in fact, it *was* my life. Almost a third of my day was spent in the classroom, and for those of us involved in sports, tack on another three hours. Grand Blanc High School provided good teachers and good coaches—a number of whom, along with classmates, became lifelong friends. Our conversations back then were face-to-face and by phone. There were no cell phones or computers, no text messages or emails and no social media. In many ways it was so much better.

As I moved from elementary to middle school and high school, classmates, teachers, and coaches increasingly dominated my life. There were a few special personalities who had a lasting impact on my life.

First and foremost, there was Robby (Jim Robinson). Robby was a huge factor in my life from our first contact in a second grade classroom to the day he died. When I first met Robby, he had transferred from the Flint Schools to Grand Blanc two weeks after school started. My recollection is that he entered the room sporting a brown corduroy suit, a red bow tie and a missing front tooth. I remember sarcastically thinking, "Isn't this kid proper!" While we had some contact in the elementary years, we didn't share teachers again until middle school. We did, however, play on the same baseball team in the Flint summer sandlot program, and many friendships started there. It wasn't until high school that we became the closest of friends.

Robby was "yin" and I was "yang." Two totally different personalities. His was a booming personality with a big smile to match. I was shy and reserved, at least until high school. He attracted attention. I shied from it. In short, we kind of balanced each other in a special way and quickly became the best of friends.

Upon graduation, Robby enrolled at Western Michigan University, I at Central Michigan University. After his freshman year, he transferred to CMU where we became roommates. The shenanigans that boy pulled off over the next three years were stuff of which legends are built.

One example stands out because it struck close to home. I was "Mr. Neatness," he was a slob. We were the *Odd Couple*'s Oscar and Felix! I continually picked up after him. One day, I returned to our room located on the third floor of the Barnes Hall only to find Robby sitting, smirking in a chair in the study area. When I entered the room we shared, I found out why. Everything I owned was in the courtyard three stories below...clothes, shoes, coats, bedding, and mattress. His message was "leave my stuff alone." Imagine my embarrassment when I had to retrieve the stuff with 160 dorm residents hooting and hollering. Quite a spectacle! Many more were Robby's exploits, but time and discretion do not permit me to share them all. You get the picture!

Bobby and "my best friend ever," Robby

After CMU, Robby was the best man at my wedding and later I was his. We were partners in officiating basketball for over 30 years. While we operated in different capacities in our careers in education, I found him to be a trusted voice. When I left the classroom to become an administrator, Robby was so gifted in sorting out personalities and problems that I found myself contacting him for advice and perspective on major issues I faced. His passing two years ago is a major reason for my writing this book. He was a force in my life like no other.

And then there was Bob Suci, the greatest athlete in the history of Grand Blanc High School. A two-time All-State athlete in football and basketball, Bob later starred in football at Michigan State University. Still later, he played professionally for the Boston Patriots (today's New England Patriots) and the Denver Broncos. Three things stand out for me about Bob. First, he was successful in any sport or activity he tried. The first time he played golf, he shot an 80 for 18 holes. The first time he put on a pair of hockey skates, he looked and played like Gordie Howe. The first time he held a tennis racquet in his hands, he beat the school's best. Second, his favorite activities above football, basketball and track were hunting and fishing. After football practice in the fall, he was off to hunt pheasants. At a championship baseball game our junior year, no one could find him before the game. He had quickly walked to a pond 50 yards away to fish. Third, in addition to being a top football, basketball, and baseball player in the state and holder of a school long jump record for many years, he was a simply wonderful classmate and friend. With all his fame, he never forgot where he came from.

Oh yeah, Bob was also an entrepreneur and in some ways a franchiser. In those days, trapping muskrats was a big deal and a good source of income. Pelts sold for $1.75. According to "Bob's law," you trapped only in the territory he established for you. To cross into *his* territory was a mortal sin. The third guy in our trio, Dennis Karas did just that and set me up. He left evidence that *I* had not only trapped in his territory but stole his traps. There was hell to pay until things were unwound!

In high school, I was our class valedictorian. The boy who helped get me there was a classmate by the name of Jack Miller. I was solid in the humanities and math, not so much in science. As my lab partner, Jack carried me through Biology, Chemistry and Physics. There was much more to Jack, however, that gained my respect. Only a few of us realized how talented an athlete he was and would have been, save for a heart condition uncovered by the Miller family doctor, a condition that precluded competition for him in our high school years. He was clearly the third best athlete in a class blessed by great athletes. Jack, true to his make-up, never complained. He suffered in silence as our teams racked up championships. He supported his teammates and me non-stop. Jack later majored in engineering at the University of Michigan and, in his adult life, was a successful partner in a thriving engineering firm.

A fourth person in my circle of closest friends was Dale Hittle, a pal through our teen years. We fell out of contact for 30 years, and then resumed our friendship late in our adult life. A son of Whigville, like me, I often kidded him that he lived in the "upper crust" of Whigville. We lived nearly a mile apart, so by bicycle, I hardly worked up a sweat going to his house. By age eight, we were close friends, and I loved to visit his house because his mother, Grace, was so nice to me. Without fail, her great cookies greeted me after coming through her door—homemade and to die for! After what could have been a bribe, she sometimes would take me aside to ask if Dale was a bad boy or in trouble anywhere. Of course, I'd throw Dale under the bus and detail his indiscretions. Getting Dale in trouble was hilarious—though I'm quite sure this was a game with his mom and the consequences were minimal or imaginary.

Dale was an exceptional athlete. Not big or fast, he had a "motor" for competition, a real drive to compete and win! He took pride in his school and in his classmates. No one was more loyal to the class of 1958 or to Grand Blanc High School than Dale. He was a dynamo of friendship and the apple didn't fall far from the tree. It was his parents who drove my mother (who never drove) to school and sporting events—sparing her the three mile walk from our house to the high school.

Then there was Lorna Lawson Green. While I have difficulty remembering what happened yesterday, I vividly remember one of my first contacts with Lorna.

It was her seventh birthday party, over seven-and-a half decades ago, December of 1947.

It may be hard for the reader to believe this, but I can remember one game we played at Lorna's birthday party. Now remember, this happened 76 years ago! The first game we played that afternoon involved a race involving cotton balls on a spoon. It was a relay race, so I had a partner. You had to walk or run with a cotton ball on a spoon to a partner who in turn would travel the course and return to you. This was done 4 times, with the winning team the first to successfully run the course. If the cotton ball fell off the spoon, you had to start all over again. My partner and I were clearly in the lead when, on the last leg, the cotton ball fell off the spoon, so we had to start all over. The winners received something of significance (which I don't recall). I was reduced to tears. For all intents and purposes the party was over for me (again, 76 years ago)! She has remained a close friend all these years.

While her high school bio reveals a person immersed in school activities, one who participated in countless clubs and organizations, what always impressed me about Lorna was her loyalty to her classmates. Any function of our class to this very day carries her fingerprints. She always did the dirty work necessary to make the activity a success. I value her friendship today as I did eight decades ago. No one defined the character and quality of the Class of 1958 more than Lorna.

I had some extraordinary mentors in my life.

While we didn't call them mentors at the time, there were several staff members at Grand Blanc High School who were tremendously influential then and as my life unfolded following high school. I can see with so much clarity now what these individuals did for me in the long trajectory of my life.

As a kid, I loved reading about American history and the characters in it, beginning with the original settlers to the pioneers who moved westward, to the characters of the Revolutionary War times, all the way through the first half of the 19th century. Luckily for me, I ran into a U.S. History teacher my junior year who would alter my life from that year forward. His name was Bill Kerensky, and his talent for teaching, coupled with my love of American history, led me to choose teaching as a career and U.S. History as my major. All great teachers bring the subject to life. He did this for me. I would like to believe that as a teacher, I mirrored his talent and passion for teaching and brought history to life for my students.

Securing his doctorate, Mr. Kerensky became a national figure in the community schools movement. On several occasions over the years, he tried to recruit me to enter this new field and become his partner in expanding the movement beyond its birthplace, Flint, Michigan. Given where community education had its genesis, I was flattered that he thought I could become a leader in the field, but I chose to remain in K-12 education. Still, we stayed in contact over the years until his passing in 2018.

Then there was my favorite principal. How many

high school students would say that one of the most impactful persons in their life in the teen years was the principal? I can for Miss Hazel Dowd, all 4'10" of her. She was in my corner throughout my high school experience. She was tough as nails, but for me a real friend and advocate.

My first contact with Miss Dowd occurred when I was in the fifth grade. I was a member of the crossing guard corps, and Miss Dowd was our sponsor. Our job was to assist students crossing at the light in front of the high school before and after school. It was an honor to be involved in this program. One of the perks in this job was to visit Greenfield Village in June following the end of the school year. Greenfield Village showcased homes and businesses of early Americana and was a major attraction to old and young alike. Miss Dowd sponsored the trip and provided transportation and food at the site. It was a great experience. She made it special.

With dedication and hard work comes promotions —and Miss Dowd was promoted to high school principal at Grand Blanc just in time for my arrival at high school. Based on our earlier contact, she took a special interest in me as I navigated those four years. As I progressed through high school, she encouraged me to look at college and at teaching as a career. It didn't take much pressure from Miss Dowd. I decided early that I wanted to be a teacher. Periodically, while at college, I would hear from her. She steadfastly supported my career choice and asked me if I would be interested in returning to my alma mater as a U.S.

History teacher. I was both interested and moved, and did return to GBHS! She later urged me to consider a career in administration. I did, and with her support, ultimately became the high school principal in the same seat she had held!

One humorous story about Miss Dowd and our friendship. In my senior year, a group of my classmates and I went deer hunting over the Thanksgiving break. On Sunday, no one wanted to go home for school on Monday. Someone had the brainstorm to call Miss Dowd and tell her we were snowed in with no hope of getting out. All looked at me, and knowing my friendship with Miss Dowd, selected me to make the call. I resisted. They threatened bodily harm! I caved in and made the call telling our principal we were snowed in with no hope of getting out. My reputation with her was sterling, so she, of course, relented and told us to stay another day. There wasn't a flake of snow on the ground! To this day I feel like I should have confessed. But time has a way of putting things in perspective. Perhaps she knew the truth. Principals do just know things!

A third person with considerable sway in my development as a kid, and a mentor in the truest sense, was Frank Thomas, our football coach. Mr. Thomas came to Grand Blanc in my freshman year. The program had been in decline for years, and Coach Thomas was hired to turn the situation around. After a dismal first year, the program took off, and in my junior and senior years, we were undefeated. Mr. Thomas believed in me and in my teammates and brought out the best in us. He helped me realize my potential as a football player, but more importantly, he believed in my potential as a boy growing into a man. How often have we heard of good coaches doing exactly that for their student athletes? Well, he did that for me and the effect went far beyond football.

Later, when I became an administrator, eventually becoming principal of Grand Blanc High School, Mr. Thomas, then the athletic director, guided and supported me at every step. He was again a teacher and coach, not to a football player, but this time to a young principal who had the responsibility to lead a high school of 3,000 students. Support, encouragement, and advice from a seasoned administrator were so critical in my growth in the position. Even in his retirement, Mr. Thomas stayed with me and continued his mentorship of a former student athlete. I often went to him for his perspective on an issue. He never failed to deliver!

The last of my four mentors from my high school days, and without question the most impactful, was again a coach. Jack Pratt was my position coach in football at GBHS. He was, then, an assistant to head coach, Frank Thomas. Mr. Pratt left our high school in the spring of 1958 to take a head coaching position. His record from that point forward places him in a win-loss record in the two major high school sports, football and basketball, with the greats of Michigan sports history.

More than any other teacher or coach he impacted my life from the time I was a high school junior till he left this earth. In high school, Mr. Pratt encouraged, prodded, and cajoled me to be a better player, but far more importantly, to be a better person. Our relationship went far beyond the football field. Mr. Pratt befriended me at every turn. For example, he and his fiancée took Robby and me to several weekend football games (we played Friday nights) with a post-game sundae or chocolate malt. I was a "cadet teacher" for him in his physical education class where I was daily mentored on life and its challenges. Mr. Pratt was the person who firmly planted in me the notion that college was not a choice but a mandate for a young man moving forward. In fact, he took Robby and me to visit Central Michigan University our junior year in high school, gave us a tour of the campus, introduced us to members of the coaching staff and, yes, took us to a diner for an ice cream treat. Later, he pressed me to apply to CMU which was only a passing thought until his high-pressure campaign. Later, I did apply and a great college education became my ticket to a better life.

When on a break from CMU, I invariably visited the Pratts (married by that time) and soaked in more of life's challenges and lessons. Whenever things "went south" in my life, he was there. At times of life's celebrations...a wedding, childbirths, promotions...he was there.

Over a span of 60 years, Mr. Pratt was a part of my life. No one outside my family had the impact of Coach Jack Pratt. His passing in September of 2012 left a huge void in my life and sealed for me—along with so many more of life's important lessons—the importance of having and being a mentor.

How lucky to have these three mentors! (Jack Pratt, Frank Thomas, Bill Kerensky 1957)

Sadly, the impact of mentors is too often underplayed. Their influence and impact is a story in itself. It certainly was in mine. Without the influence of these four significant individuals, my life could well have followed a different, and less successful, course. I have often reflected on my good fortune, that I was in the right place at the right time relative to the quality of my mentors. My life track confirms this. I have been blessed. At the same time, with great blessings come great opportunities for growth and accomplishment. It was time to launch into making a difference in the lives of others, like so many had done for me.

5

BACK TO GRAND BLANC HIGH
SCHOOL...& BEYOND

FROM MY 10TH GRADE FORWARD, I knew I was going to be a teacher. I loved my experience in K-12 education. The formative years of kindergarten through the 6th grade set the table for what was to come. My teachers at that level were, bless their collective souls, tough, demanding and definitely "old school." They were also, while they would deny it if they were alive today, sensitive, compassionate, loving human beings. I could, if asked, describe each of them in some detail. I loved all five of them. I say five because after one week of kindergarten, I was transferred for some unknown reason, to a first grade classroom. In the grand scheme of things, the move worked out well for me, except for one unforeseen consequence. I was to be a 16-year-old senior playing varsity football on a powerhouse team loaded with strong, aggressive 18-year-olds...a definite disadvantage!

My junior high years were a blur. I'm not sure why,

but perhaps it was the onset of adolescence, just the big change from elementary school, or the fact that it was just two years, seventh and eighth grades. Whatever the case, it was in high school that I blossomed as a student, an athlete and a leader. I loved those four years!

In addition to the challenge of the classroom, there were a multitude of experiences for any student including clubs, sports, music and the theater, as well as the opportunity to meet new people and take on new challenges. I was all in. In high school, I met teachers and coaches who had a profound impact on my life going forward. In my instance, I drew from them in ways that unconsciously pointed me toward the possibility of a career in teaching.

By the end of my junior year, I was certain that I wanted to be a teacher. Mr. Kerensky, my U.S. History teacher, and Mr. Pratt, my football coach, helped guide my thinking about the potential of teaching as a career choice. Both were Central Michigan University graduates, so they soon made it clear they felt CMU was the place to pursue a teaching degree. Go Chips!

So five years after completing high school, August of 1963, I graduated from CMU with BA and MA degrees. Earlier that spring, I began the interview process for a teaching position in the Flint area. Jobs were readily available due to the baby boom of the 1940s and early 1950s. After weeks of interviews, I narrowed my choice to two suburban Flint school systems, Grand Blanc, my alma mater, and Carman-Ainsworth. Interestingly, several of my friends and even some former teachers advised against Grand Blanc using the old adage, "you can't go home again." I had been a little nervous about returning to Grand Blanc, anyway. I made the decision to interview with both schools.

Quickly, everything pointed to Carman-Ainsworth, specifically Ainsworth High School. They offered a full schedule of teaching U.S. History, my major, plus coaching jobs in football and baseball. The school system was experiencing rapid growth in student population, so there was no danger of losing a job due to declining numbers.

However, a glitch developed. When I went in for the final interview, to my surprise it featured a tour of the high school by none other than the Superintendent. I was initially impressed that the head person was conducting the tour, but the early enthusiasm soured as we were touring the building. On three separate occasions, he called a teacher out of his classroom into the hallway where I stood. He loudly chastised each teacher as I stood nearby. One teacher was sitting on his desk as we passed his classroom, another had a coffee cup in his hand and a third did not have a shirt and tie. None of these constituted a cardinal sin in my judgment. The teachers were visibly shaken. My first thought was why did he do this in front of me? Either he wanted to prove to me how tough he was or that he had high expectations for his employees. It had the opposite outcome in either case. I felt incredibly offended. At that time, the tour could have been terminated.

The very next day, I called my former high school principal, and the person who recruited me, Miss Dowd, to tell her I wanted to return to Grand Blanc—I hit the right chord. She was very excited and very emotional over the phone. That was what I needed at that point, plus they offered an elementary teaching job to my wife, Sally. We signed contracts two days later. Grand Blanc was the right choice despite my earlier misgivings.

For the moment, however, there was chaos. We were in mid-August, our first child was a month old, the start of school in Grand Blanc was three weeks away and we had to move from Mt. Pleasant to Grand Blanc without having secured housing in Grand Blanc. Not to worry! On that following Monday, we rented a U-Haul, gathered all of our possessions (few in number) in the storage area and drove to my parents' house as temporary housing. The next day we began looking for a rental home. Three days later we hit gold but with an interesting twist. There were three other couples looking at the house we wanted, but the owner took a liking to us and awarded us the house. There was one caveat, however. Besides paying the first three months of rent, we had to agree to paint the entire interior of the home before Thanksgiving. Together we faced a major move, with a newborn, Sally and I beginning our careers in two weeks and a house to paint. We made it happen!

What followed was a career of 38 years, principally in three school districts: Grand Blanc, Clarkston and Fenton. For 21 years my employment was with the

Grand Blanc Community Schools. Sally and I were young, as were our colleagues and friends. Those were the best of times.

I began my career in Grand Blanc in 1963 as a U.S. History teacher and coach. The district was growing by leaps and bounds, and the high school by 1975 was the third largest in the state. I thoroughly enjoyed teaching and planned on that being my entire career until a new principal, Howard Clayton, entered the scene in 1966. A year later, he asked me if I would consider a jump to administration as an assistant principal. I told him I hadn't considered a move from the classroom, but I would give it a try. So in 1967 I became an administrative intern, followed the next year by selection as a full-time assistant principal. Following my fourth year as an assistant, Mr. Clayton confided in me he was taking a job as assistant superintendent with the district and would I consider applying for the building principalship. Again, I hadn't given it much thought—I was really happy in my current post and Mr. Clayton had allowed me to do some coaching. After discussing the possibility with Sally, I decided to throw my hat in the ring. I applied for the job of principal at Grand Blanc High School (GBHS).

The position was very attractive because of the size and reputation of both the high school and the community in which we lived. Grand Blanc had become an attractive bedroom community for the legions of General Motors employees who flooded the area in the 1960s, '70s and '80s. Somewhat to my surprise, because of the pedigree of the candidates who applied for the job, I was awarded the position, the best job I ever held in public education. The year was 1972, and for the next 12 years, I served as Principal of GBHS.

A rookie principal at work, Grand Blanc High School '72-'73

Those were electric years for me and for GBHS. A great young staff, wonderful students, supportive parents and a great community all combined to make this one of the best high schools in southeast Michigan. I was 31 years old when I assumed the position. Fortunately for me, I was able to secure talented assistants. I believe that was one of the hallmarks of my tenure as principal in Grand Blanc. Year by year we hired young, talented, and driven individuals to the position of assistant principal. Many of them with just a few years of experience in Grand Blanc left to become high school principals or central office administrators in other districts.

There were certainly issues we had to face during my 12 years as principal of GBHS. Labor problems, financial downturns, even an all school walkout wouldn't mar my years there. For more than a decade of my time as principal, we were one of the premier high schools in Michigan, a position held to this day.

Did this team really lead the high school?
(GBHS early '80s)

One of the important features of my years as principal was the impact of senior district administrators on my personal growth. The man who preceded me as principal, Howard Clayton, the superintendent at the time, Jim Burchyett and his assistant, Ed Crandall, were among the group who took off the rough edges of a young principal. Those years at GBHS, where I spent the major share of my 38 years in public education, marked the years of my greatest growth as a leader, paving the way for the remaining two major stopping points in my career.

The first of those stops came in Clarkston. I knew very little about the high school when I applied for the high school principalship in the spring of 1986. I knew something of the community, which had an outstanding reputation, but little else. At the time of my application, I had served the preceding two years as a superintendent in a small district southwest of Flint. I wasn't happy with the results of those years and especially displeased with my performance, so I was determined to get back to my roots as a high school principal, where I had experienced success. I actually applied for two positions, both as high school principal, at Davison and Clarkston. I was offered both jobs. I chose to go to Clarkston.

The high school had recently been through difficult times with three principals in two years. Not a good sign. While I didn't officially begin my tenure until July 1, 1986, I decided to attend the graduation ceremony in June of that year, a month before I officially became principal. One can learn a lot about a high school by observing their graduation. The site was Pine Knob Amphitheater in Clarkston. The evening was a disaster. The male grads were poorly dressed for the occasion with significant numbers of them walking with open gowns and wearing Bermuda shorts. Many didn't have shoes on. Beach balls were bounced around everywhere throughout the ceremony. Vulgar words were tossed out by several as they crossed the stage.

The following day I went to the high school to observe the underclassmen leaving the building. It was both disappointing and telling. A good hundred students were involved in a shaving cream fight at the front of the building. Many were smoking cigarettes. Firecrackers were exploding in the parking lot. I am being generous when I say both events were a disaster.

I knew then why I was being hired. The Board of Education wanted a "sheriff," and while I knew getting the high school under control was important, restoring the faith of parents and the community in its high school was to be equally important.

The good news is that there was no way to move except up as school resumed in the fall. I knew enough about leadership that certain conditions had to be present for me to be successful in turning things around. Among them were a supportive Board of Education and an equally supportive superintendent. I pulled no punches when I met with them in our initial session in July. I told them tough decisions had to be made, and they would be challenged on occasion to support me, but support me they must. Fortunately they did so whenever called on. Convincing a dubious staff was the next challenge. They were a beleaguered lot when I met with them that last day of school. Without exaggeration, they had gone through "hell" the previous two years.

The first year was tough. It was difficult to change the negative behavior and attitude of many youngsters, mostly seniors. They saw me as the next principal to run out of town. Without going through the details, we did turn around the situation in one year, not without some pain on their part and mine. The staff was magnificent in responding to the challenge. Over the first semester of the year, major progress was made, leading to a really positive school environment the last half of the school year.

The next four years in Clarkston were a success story on all fronts. So much credit belongs to district leadership, the teaching staff and the great majority of students who the previous year had to endure the antics of a small but active minority bent on chaos.

Encouraged by improvement, I was very happy in Clarkston with no desire to leave as I completed my fifth year in June of 1991. One day a colleague from my days in Grand Blanc, then an administrator in the Fenton Schools, called me early in May asking if I would be interested in the superintendent position of that district. While I was very happy in Clarkston, there was something about the opportunity that intrigued me. Remember, I had gone back to my success as a high school principal in taking the Clarkston job. The thought of returning to a superintendent position and succeeding at that level had a special attraction for me. I needed to demonstrate to myself that I was capable of succeeding at the district level. I subsequently applied for the position of Fenton Superintendent.

For some reason the process to select a new superintendent lagged over the summer months. It wasn't until August that the interviews concluded, and I was selected as the new Superintendent of the Fenton

Schools. By then, my attention was focused on opening Clarkston High School, pre-Labor Day. Now I had to balance the Clarkston situation with starting a new position in Fenton. As it turned out, it wasn't such a challenge, because the Fenton Schools were in the middle of a teacher strike.

Some history: In 1966, the State of Michigan passed legislation opening the dam for collective bargaining for public entities; thus, Michigan teachers could bargain for salary and benefits and classified staff could as well. Fenton staff took it to the extreme. Both groups had gone on strike every three years from 1966 until the day I started the job in 1991.

I told the Fenton Board that due to the lateness of my selection, I felt obligated to open school in Clarkston pre-Labor Day. I would then join Fenton the following week. In reality, I was with Fenton administrative staff devising a strategy to settle another teacher strike. We worked over the Labor Day weekend, and the strike was settled within a week. I was a hero in the community (and with the staff), but in reality a lot of good people came together to bring this disruption to an end.

My tenure in Fenton over the next 10 years was a successful one. There were a myriad of challenges, not the least of which was restoring trust between the board and district staff, and between the school district and the community. Parents weren't the only target group. The community at large, including businesses, law enforcement, city and township offices and senior citizens all felt ignored or neglected. No one from the district sought their advice or input. This breakdown with the community was the first order of business.

In short, we did restore faith within and outside the school community. Trust was an important byproduct of this effort. Other issues inside the district were addressed as well. Student performance, those all important test scores, improved dramatically over the ensuing years. A decadent K-12 arts program was a priority and significant gains were achieved including major advances in staffing at all levels. Partnerships between community groups and the district were a major focus, the most important of which was a monthly meeting between district and city government officials. The results were more than noteworthy.

The day I left the district, the president of the teachers' union asked to see me. I anticipated a handshake and a wish to enjoy retirement. In fact he said, "You did something I didn't think possible. We trusted you. You restored integrity and honesty to the position." That might be the nicest compliment I ever received.

Looking back, what does all this mean? How did circumstances, events, and people influence my life, my successes and failures, my growth? My mind naturally gravitates to three formative buckets. I'll call the first one *Growing Up in Whigville.* The second I'll refer to as the *Evolution of Leadership Style.* The third I'll name *The Blessing of Problems and Challenges,* and by this I mean the unique problems I faced in the three school districts I served the majority of my time in K-12 education.

Growing Up in Whigville

First, I am a kid from blue collar Whigville! It was a very special lower-middle-class community. From there—and in large part because of the people and my beginnings there—I was able to rise to the highest level of K-12 public school administration. I was not a child from affluence given all the resources and support in the world to succeed as an adult. Mine was a lower-middle-class family, but one with loving parents who gave all they had to their children so that they could forge a better life. They inspired, challenged, and supported me. I can name a few friends from my neighborhood who went on to college and then into various professions...law, business, medicine, or education. However, the vast majority went directly from high school to good paying labor or skilled-trades jobs in one of the General Motors plants in the Flint area. My heart was somewhere else and my neighborhood, K-12 experience, and parents gave me everything I needed to find my way.

Even so, I never had a clear goal to lead in education. I simply wanted to teach and coach. At all the steps on the way to the superintendent position, I never aspired to be an assistant principal, a principal, or even, ultimately, superintendent. The jobs came to me. People nurtured me and circumstances fell my way. As I reflect on my career, I'm amazed that I never had a clear game plan to ascend the ladder in my profession. It just happened.

As far back as I can remember, I inevitably found myself in leadership positions—whether back in the neighborhood in pick-up sports, as president of my class all four years in high school, or captaining the athletic teams. Leadership, or the responsibilities and expectations that come with it, have never been foreign to me. I embraced leadership and the accompanying duties.

Evolution of Leadership Style

Lately, I've been given to reflection on how my approach to leadership evolved over the years and how I see myself 20 years later. I grew and changed over time. How I related to kids, parents, and teachers from the 1960s till the end of my career in 2001 transformed through the fires of the changing times and the needs of students. I am convinced my leadership style was significantly molded by the changes in society beginning in the 1950s.

In the 1950s and the preceding decades, leadership was top down in society. In education, leaders operated on that model. Administrators told principals and principals told teachers how the building and programs would function. The same principle applied in the home. Child-raising was decidedly "top-down." Children didn't question their parents or other adults in their lives. I can recall as a child being told at family gatherings to be seen and not heard. Even in a reasonably progressive family like the Bureks, little input was sought from me or my sister when it came to decisions affecting our lives.

Expectations of teachers were clearly defined by the principal with little input from staff. That applied to key decisions impacting staff, including salary and benefits. Day-to-day operation for staff was dictated by principals and the Board of Education.

All of this began to change in the 1960s. That decade saw a social revolution that upended the relationship between adults and children in the family and between Boards of Education, administrators and teachers in the buildings.

Kids in the 1960s rebelled against the "my way or the highway" approach. As a beginning teacher in 1963, I struggled with this change. Kids said and did things that they wouldn't have said or done in the 1950s. I recall talking to a 1967 graduate about the change. He was a very bright, articulate young man who could have functioned equally well in the 1950s or '60s. He said, "Dr. Burek, the 1950s kid thought about speaking up and speaking out. He simply didn't do it—the 1960s kid did." As a teacher, I had to alter my approach in order to survive. The authoritarian approach did not work in the 1960s classroom.

An incident occurred halfway through my first year as principal of Grand Blanc High School. The year was 1973, significant because it came in the hotbed that was dissent over the Vietnam War. While attention largely focused on college campuses, the anti-war message filtered down to high schools. We

had the previous summer beefed up the student attendance policy. It came across as mean-spirited to our
students. As it was implemented in the fall of my first
year as principal, students cried about how unfair it
was. In retrospect, they were right. Finally, at the
beginning of the second semester, students en masse
bolted the building...the entire student body. That
night, I told my wife that my tenure as principal was
probably over. Fortunately, the Superintendent called
me that same night and assured me that he and the
Board of Education were totally in my corner! No
more comforting words were ever issued!

I learned that teachers were professionals and
yearned to be included in decisions. When I became
an administrator in 1968, my approach to staff had to
respond to this attending to society's changes. Those
students from the 1960s became teachers in that
decade and beyond. The authoritarian approach
didn't resonate with teachers any more than it did
with students. No longer could a superintendent
dictate salary or working conditions without involve-
ment of teachers. The world was changing.

I grew up in the 1950s, became a teacher in the
early 1960s. All of these changes in the workplace had
a profound impact on me. As I adjusted to the "new
norm," I believe I became a better teacher and, later, a
better principal. I believe my leadership style recognized and incorporated the changes in society. Not
doing so would have relegated me to becoming an
average teacher without the tools to grow into an

effective leader. I became a good teacher and a good administrator because I changed with the times.

The Blessings of Problems and Challenges

Our problems and challenges become the furnace where the tools of leadership are forged. I was changed by the unique problems I faced in each of the three districts I served. I had never really given much thought to this theme, but in anticipation of writing this book, it quickly evolved as I got deeper into this process.

Grand Blanc first up. Of course, I had some idea of what I was getting into when I took the position of principal at GBHS. I had grown up in Grand Blanc, attended the schools K-12, and taught four years before first becoming assistant principal (1968-1972), and four years later principal of the high school for 12 years (1972-1984). During my assistant principal years, the number of new students grew beyond anyone's expectations.

When I graduated from GBHS in 1958, there were 500 students, grades 9-12. By 1975, 17 years later, the high school numbered 2,903 students. So the challenges were there on multiple fronts. In no particular order, the major challenges were: (1) hiring staff; (2) updating a stagnant curriculum for a new generation of students; (3) student control issues; and (4) meeting the expectations of the Superintendent and Board of Education and a very aggressive parent community.

As an assistant principal, I didn't carry home each

night the weight of these expectations. As the principal, I went to bed each night and woke up each morning thinking about them. I knew that making the right decisions would determine our success as a high school and my future as a leader, then and for years to come.

I must note that we were blessed with a great teaching staff, strong, competent assistant principals, an outstanding student body and amazingly supportive parents.

When I left GBHS in 1984, I knew we were one of the very best high schools in southeast Michigan, a tradition that carries on to this day.

Relative to Clarkston High School the building had gone through three principals in 18 months. I was the fourth. I knew from experience that "cracking down" wasn't the only action needed. Students in general had to know that I was their #1 cheerleader. While the staff and I would deal with the foolishness of a fairly large group of senior boys, there were other "fish to fry." So, yes, getting the place under control was job one.

By the end of the year, I felt we were in a good place with kids and staff. There were bumps along the road to be sure, but I was able to bring the experience of two decades of leadership of a huge high school to Clarkston High School. In reality, the socioeconomic base of the two communities was very similar and so were the kids.

Equally important, we were able to engage parents and community in meaningful ways. This included "coffees" at over 20 homes to get firsthand their feelings about the high school, to creating an advisory council that represented the diversity of the community, to organizing a parent support group, numbering over 100 parents, arranged into multiple committees, all serving the high school. So while student misbehavior was the tip of the iceberg in terms of problems, it ceased to be an issue after one year. Engaging parents and the community were major efforts to restore confidence in the high school. This became the priority on my first day on the job.

My superintendency in Fenton, on the surface, was all about labor problems, but there were other issues of equal significance. Parents felt neglected. The community was not engaged in any meaningful way. In my initial year on the job we focused on trust and communication. The environment became more inclusive so that staff felt respected with a willingness on my part to engage issues in a collaborative way. This approach was introduced to the community as well. Since all five district buildings were located in the City of Fenton, we immediately reached out to City officials and we engaged the Chamber of Commerce. Our physical presence at community events was a priority. I'm proud to say when I retired in 2001, there was a very positive spirit in the district and in the community.

The history of these experiences fascinates me to this day. After serving as a leader in three districts with a diversity of problems and challenges, I can say they were always met with the help and support of many in each community. It always came down to a leader willing to listen and help sort out the issues and a community willing to address our challenges together. I feel blessed to have had a role in all of this, but so many others also deserve the credit. In my retirement years, I reflect often on special people and good memories from three great districts and the communities they served. Whether or not we are aware of it, we're all leaving a legacy. We should try to leave a good one.

6

A LEGACY OF LEADERSHIP

AFTER EIGHTY-THREE YEARS on the face of this earth and thirty-eight years as a public school teacher and administrator, it is time to reflect on a life and career spanning nine decades. I do so with no illusion that there is something unique or special or groundbreaking in my story—who I am or what I have accomplished—but I do believe it is a story worth telling.

Anyone who has examined my story, the early years in the neighborhood in which I was raised, might have imagined a totally different trajectory. They would not have predicted that this baseball-playing, fur-trapping boy would one day earn his doctorate degree or become the principal of what is now the second largest high school in Michigan. They would not have projected "Bobby" Burek (as I was called as a kid growing up) as a lock to one day become the superintendent of a quality K-12 school system. They likely would have predicted that after high school graduation (if I achieved a diploma at all) I would, as did so many of my Whigville peers, take a job as an assembler at Chevrolet, Buick Motors or AC Spark Plug and put in 30 years of work before retiring in my early 50s.

The typical career path for boys of my generation coming out of the dirt roads of Whigville, found them living a different life, a life that included laboring as an autoworker, marrying at a very young age and raising a large family. It also, because of lucrative wages supplemented by generous overtime pay, would have them living a very good life including a nice home in the suburbs and a summer cottage in northern Michigan. Perhaps owning a fishing boat, two snowmobiles and the best hunting and fishing equipment money could buy. So many of my childhood friends lived this exact life—a good life, but not my life. Somebody needs to be the teacher, the coach, the principal, the change-agent leader. A seemingly unlikely trajectory for a boy from Whigville, but I am blessed that this has been mine and I got to be entrusted with the education of the children of automobile workers, construction workers, laborers, store owners and so many others. I am of all people, most blessed.

I could have been an autoworker. I did not follow this path for a number of reasons, not the least of which was the idea of working eight hours a day assembling the same part in the same way. I respect those who made this sacrifice for their families. Most found other outlets and interests outside of work. I was "built" to be immersed in my work life. Education provided this life for me. I had two wonderful parents who recognized this and wanted something better for their children and were willing to sacrifice their lives to that end. There is no doubt that without their unwavering support, my life would have taken a different turn.

An equally strong push for me to do better, and to go to college, came from a chorus of high school teachers and coaches who pressured me to become a professional, to be a doctor, lawyer, engineer, businessman or, yes, a teacher. I believe without this push coming from the adults I encountered in high school, I would not have gone to college to become a teacher.

So now as life closes in, what is my legacy? This is the time for honest reflection. I will be very candid and very critical in self-reflection, my personal assessment of the impact my life has had on the small piece of the universe in which I lived and worked. I also want to first offer some thoughts on how I believe I functioned as a husband and father.

First, the family side. I have been blessed with an incredible wife and three wonderful daughters. I believe Sally would describe me as a good husband, a very good husband. As a breadwinner, she would say I did well. No one who goes into education gets rich, but it can be a very comfortable living. More importantly, I believe she would say that I am a very caring, loving husband, father and grandfather. She would also say that I adore her because I do and have done so as we approach the 62nd year of marriage.

An earlier chapter described our first meeting and subsequent courtship. Nothing has changed in our marriage. I love her now as I did then. Sally would say that I put her and family first, because I did. She would also say, in a moment of candor, that I am a workaholic and perfectionist, and those qualities sometimes challenged our marriage. Finally, respect enters into the equation, and this is and always has been mutual. I respect her as a wife, mother and grandmother and she, in turn, respects me.

What is my legacy with my daughters? I have loved Melissa, Amy and Wendy and worshipped them from the day they were born. I believe they would say the same about their father. In the order of the universe, girls gravitate to their dads, especially during those difficult teen years, and boys do the same with their mothers. In good times, and not so good times, I have always been there for them. A good listener I am, and that quickly endeared me to our daughters.

It was very difficult for me to see them enter adulthood and leave the house, but I honestly believe our relationship has only gotten stronger as they became young adults, went to college, got married and gave us seven beautiful grandchildren. While we live miles apart, the frequent phone calls and less frequent visits hold the relationships together as they move into the second half of their lives.

Next my legacy on the professional side of my life. My experience in the three districts in which I worked showcased my ability to define major issues facing the building or district and providing the leadership to solve them. Easy to describe, difficult to accomplish, but accomplish we did. In Grand Blanc the major issues revolved around managing historic growth in student numbers but also placing focus on students. The staff had to be convinced to change building priorities to put the emphasis on young adults. In Clarkston, on its face it was student misbehavior, but first we had to gain the confidence of the other 95% of students plus the staff, parents and community as well. No small task. In Fenton, labor relations were clearly the major issue, but getting staff and parents to trust me was key to our success.

FENTON HIGH SCHOOL
"Commencement Ceremony"
June 2, 1993

Fenton High School, a legacy of leadership

In my entire life, I have demonstrated an ability to lead. From the days of my childhood in the neighborhood, kids looked to me for leadership. In the formal school setting, that confidence continued. I was the leader of several clubs, president of our student council, and president of my class all four years of high school. My friends and classmates looked to me for leadership at the next level. In college I led clubs, was president of our dormitory council, and captained the baseball team. Why? I like people...I respect them. I listened carefully to any person willing to voice an opinion or concern. I involved anyone wanting to be part of the solution. I gained their confidence and, therefore, their support.

Trust and tenacity don't get enough attention when speaking of effective leadership. Trust is the currency of leadership. If people trust you, they will follow your lead. I never misled people. I never manipulated them. I never took advantage of them. If people believe in you, trust in you, they will literally "go to the wall" for you, because they know you will do the same for them. Tenacity, or toughness, is a critical element in leadership because the leader and the group will face adversity at some point. The leader will help the group look at adversity as simply one more challenge to overcome rather than the first step to defeat.

I have often said the best job to get is when the organization is at its lowest, when people have lost hope, when trust is missing, when backstabbing is rampant, when there is no direction or hope. There is only one direction, and that is up. If you can provide leadership, success is around the corner. Conversely, inheriting a great team or a great organization or a successful group of any kind is only a maintenance issue.

So this is my legacy. The ability to lead. The ability to bring people together to solve a problem, attack an issue, restore confidence in the organization. That is why I have always been in a position of leadership. Demonstrating tenacity and a can-do attitude in the face of adversity is part of my very fiber. People believed in me. They bought into my leadership.

Grand Blanc High School and Beyond

This is what I have learned about myself over a career of four decades. Leaders know it is all about people. It is not about Xs and Os or organizational charts or slogans. I learned that at an early age and never looked back. It served me well. I hope this earth is a little better because of what I have accomplished. That is my legacy, a well-documented history of leadership. The torch has now been passed to the next generation.

I hope this memoir inspires you to pick up your own torch, putting to work your own unique gifts. I hope I've helped cast a little light for you. If I've touched your life, I have been honored to do so. Many of you have touched mine. Indeed, so many faces pass in front of my mind as I write this. As for me, I'm thankful for health even as with a sense of intentionality I begin to finish some things—and it is with much joy and gratitude that I intentionally pass my still-lit torch to my angels.

7

MY EARTH ANGELS

I saw the angel in the marble and carved until I set him free. -Michelangelo

IN MY CASE my angels were all women, and they were set free, free to enjoy a life of love, joy, and purpose! I originally intended to devote this chapter to our "Earth Angels," our three daughters, but I can't pass an opportunity to devote time and space to my other angel and their mother, Sally, my "copilot" for 62 years of marriage and counting. More to follow on the girls, but first a few words about their mother, my first earth angel.

Sally has been my partner for all or part of seven decades. It was love at first sight for me at Central Michigan University. After 61 years of marriage, I can safely say if there is a kinder, more positive, more loving or sensitive or caring person, I've never met that person, not even close. Sally is the perfect woman. You could debate this point, but you'd lose. My case is overwhelming! She has never issued a negative word or unkind statement about anyone. This has been said about many, but with Sally it's true. She would never deliberately hurt another person. Heck, she has never raised her voice to me. What Sally has given to me in our marriage is true partnership in life's challenges. And she has been the hero protagonist in raising our three wonderful girls. She has patiently supported an ambitiously driven, upwardly mobile husband—and successfully pursued a career of her own once the girls were on their way in school and life.

Sally has always kept me grounded, thereby ensuring that I never got too far ahead of myself. She kept me humble, yet let me "spread my wings." Whenever I was down, she brought me back. She always knew what to say or do that was right for the moment in terms of my emotional balance.

There was a time in my life when things really came crashing down for me personally and professionally when I took my first school superintendency. A major career move seriously backfired because I wasn't quite ready for it. Until that point every move forward had met with success and praise. Not this time.

Though never professionally diagnosed, I'm sure I was in clinical depression. It was truly a perilous time for me, but I recovered in large measure because of Sally's love and support. So much of what happened in those months only strengthened our marriage. She gave me the space, love and support to care quickly for my emotional wounds and map a positive course forward. A well-known author has written masterfully about failing forward. I believe Sally knew the formula first. She was my guardian angel.

My Earth Angels Wendy, Amy, Melissa

And now to our other angels. Sally and I are blessed with three wonderful daughters. From oldest to youngest, they are Melissa, Amy and Wendy. All three had great childhoods, all three graduated from Grand Blanc High School (GBHS), their father's alma mater. I turned down numerous job offers during that time because Sally and I placed a high value on the girls' capacity to live stable lives residing in one community, going to school in one district, K-12, and graduating from GBHS.

Following graduation from high school, all three went to college: Melissa to University of Michigan;

Amy to Michigan State University; and Wendy to Notre Dame. As one might surmise, with three very competitive girls, the school rivalries for them were intense, especially when it came to football! Trash talking was at a premium. Phone exchanges after a game should have been censored! Were those my daughters?

Once through college, they went their separate ways. Following a brief but important career launch at Ford Motor Company, Melissa joined an executive compensation firm located in New York City, where she has achieved partner status in the company.

Amy, who now lives in Chicago, began her career with General Motors Parts Division, after which she decided that marriage and family would take front stage. She and her husband, Michael, are parents of two sons and a daughter.

Our youngest, Wendy, followed a path similar to sister Amy. She worked with the Arthur Anderson Accounting firm before marrying and having children. Wendy and her husband, also named Michael, are very proud parents of four boys.

From the beginning, the importance of family has been the lifeblood of our household, and our girls thrived in this environment from an early age. Our daily life was fueled with love, joy, and support for each other. Sally was the heart and soul of our journey of life, and if I may say it, I have so loved being part of the beautiful rhythm of our family. Our girls have carried this rhythm into their own families so that it has become part of a generational spirit of support and togetherness. In a word, family.

The Chicago girls have done an amazing job of raising their children who are now young adults. They have totally invested in their kids, from the moment they entered the world. Through the ensuing years, the theme and spirit of family was central to the Thompson and Locascio families. Their children received that message early and often—transmitted through unconditional love. Amy and Wendy, and their husbands, have been totally involved in the lives of their children. They raised parental attendance at school and community functions in which the kids were involved to a new level. They stressed the importance of meal times and family celebrations as "must show" events. They also stressed the importance of siblings supporting each other, solidifying family cohesion, and took joy in observing the fruits of their efforts.

Sally and I, as well as Aunt Melissa, have taken great joy in loving and supporting our Chicago families with frequent visits. Sally and I have trekked to the Windy City every month to celebrate birthdays and holidays, and Aunt Melissa has been equally committed. Well, truth is, it would be difficult to find an aunt anywhere more dedicated to her siblings' kids. What a major, positive force she has been in their lives. In fact, Melissa's commitment to her niece and nephews continues to this day. Three of the nephews, now college graduates and gainfully employed, moved in the past two years to New York City where Melissa currently lives. She moved quickly to support them. The assistance ranged from counsel on the dangers of NYC and where to go and not go, to inviting them to use the facilities in her gym membership, to lunches and dinners on Aunt Missy to check on them when health issues arose. The young men appreciate her support.

I want to take a moment to talk about one of our favorite places, an idyllic place that nurtured togetherness and family. The story of Silver Lake in Fenton should be shared here because it says so much about the Burek family. During the years I served as Superintendent of Schools in Fenton, Sally and I lived on Silver Lake, a picturesque body of water on the west side of Fenton, Michigan.

In the early years, before grandchildren entered the picture, our daughters made the 4th of July the focus of their summer. They came to town and invited friends from both their high school and college days to join them. It was a fun-filled day, and for some, a fun-filled week.

Later, when our daughters' children came onstage, the list of invitees changed. Now the focus was on family. The kids and the grandkids absolutely loved the lake, and it was a rare weekend in June, July or August in the summers of the 1990s and 2000s that one family or the other wasn't in town to visit grandma and grandpa. Over those wonderful summers, we saw the kids grow up before our very eyes.

The week of July 4th took on a special meaning in

those years. All three daughters, the children and the in-laws were with us for five to seven days. Something was happening all the time from daybreak until the middle of the night. The lake was the focus but ongoing games, a nightly campfire and fireworks on the 4th of July were featured. Swimming and boat rides, jet skis, and water skiing were nonstop events.

It wasn't until the kids were in their mid-teens that interest in the lake waned and the peer group back in Chicago appealed more to the younger generation. We nurtured growth, and with growth comes change. This is both the wonderful joy and deep melancholy of life. We must embrace both, and in this embrace are memories.

So many wonderful memories of those years are shared whenever the family gets together. It was truly a glorious time for people of all ages, and at one time it seemed it would never end...until it did.

Now that we are in our 80s, and with health issues mounting, the visits to Chicago are no longer possible. The contacts and ever-increasing support from our girls are a mainstay of our relationships. Daily telephone calls are a welcome lifeline. Melissa and Amy visit us on a monthly basis. Family circumstances don't permit Wendy to do so, but she visits as much as possible. The result is that we see our daughters often. Whenever surgeries or prolonged hospital stays are scheduled, we can expect all three girls to be present.

Thus, we continue to play a significant role in the lives of our three girls and vice versa. Our grandchildren even get involved in the act. A weekly call from each of them is a staple of our relationship. It's pretty amazing, now that six of the seven are in their 20s.

What I have chronicled in this chapter is a living definition of "angels." Melissa, Amy, and Wendy are truly angels on earth. While the girls' relationship with us has evolved in many ways, there is a constancy to that relationship. Love and respect show themselves in every way. Our lives intersect with them every day. Daughters who have for over a half century given us uncompromising love. No parent can wish for more. We are truly blessed. And Sally is my very own Earth Angel, my very heart and soul.

AFTERWORD

I have learned some important lessons in life and you've just read about many of them. I've learned as much through failure as I have success—maybe more. I've been blessed with great mentors who have helped clear the path for me and helped me interpret the lessons learned along the way.

So for what it's worth, I offer this afterword as an abridged but prioritized list of the major lessons I've learned in four decades of leadership—lessons of life and leadership. Permit me to share them with you here as principles you may choose to integrate into your own life.

1. Keep your family first. Family is who you go home to for peace and joy. Be an active builder of peace and joy in your family. You can only do this by intentionally making your family your top priority.

2. Surround yourself with good people—people with good ethics, people who are kind, people who are wise or yearn to be.

3. Know that the culture you create will impact people and decisions throughout whatever organization you lead—large or small. Every organization soon takes on the personality of its leader—for good or ill.

4. Don't retreat from challenges. Embrace them. How you perform in the face of challenges will be your calling card with the team you lead. It will define your legacy.

5. Be a good listener. As Stephen Covey famously taught, "Seek first to understand, then to be understood." Listening is an act of giving.

6. Delegate tasks as a means of survival, but recognize the strengths and weaknesses of the people to whom you delegate those tasks. Coach your people up; let their growth bring you joy.

7. Never shy from the truth. Your response in the face of an inconvenient truth will define you as a leader. Progress toward improvement and success always starts with the truth, and your integrity rests there.

8. Visibility and accessibility...so critical to your success. Be visible and accessible. Success never comes to a leader who hides.

9. Loyalty is important but only to a point. Be loyal to those who are genuine or want to learn. Do not continue to invest in those who are committed to selfishness.

10. Finally, as my dear mother repeatedly told me, "Say 'may I help you?' and 'thank you' to foe and friend alike."

ABOUT THE AUTHOR

Dr. Robert Burek was born toward the end of 1940 in Flint, Michigan, during its heyday as an automobile manufacturing powerhouse and in the tumult of the Second World War. His family moved to Detroit for a time, then back to the Flint area to a little slice of Midwest Americana known to the locals as Whigville. It was in a small, lower-middle-class neighborhood of Whigville known as The Heights that family, sand-lot baseball, fur trapping and trading, and shenanigans with a myriad of characters formed the personality, values, and skills that set Bob on a path to become an accomplished education leader, devoted husband and father, and tireless community advocate. He received his Bachelor of Arts degree from Central Michigan University, majoring in US history, in 1962. The following year, he received his Master of Arts degree from CMU, again majoring in US history. In 1976, he received his doctorate from Michigan State University, majoring in K-12 Education Administration. Bob and his wife Sally raised three daughters and have shared many extraordinary adventures together in their marriage of over 60 years!

Made in the USA
Columbia, SC
05 August 2024

40062946R00057